Demise
The Temporary Restraining Order,
the Hearsay Rule and the 2nd Amendment

Intro

My story begins in the middle of the trial to make Sam's temporary restraining order permanent. Sam testified under oath:

> "I didn't claim Christy called me on the phone every six months …the police misstated …that is just a discrepancy."

Sam's statement was in contrast to what was initially claimed in his police report that stripped me of my right to bear arms.

Sam was a 6', slender young man who filed a police report after I recently called him one day to ask him to come forward about our auto accident 7 years ago. In response, he filed for a temporary restraining order with allegations, including that I threatened his process server with a gun 7 years earlier and sexual harassment.

While listening to Sam, I could see his process server from the corner of my eye. Sam hired this tall, hearty man 7 years ago to serve me with his small claims law suit regarding our auto accident, for which he won a Default judgment when I was 5 minutes late. Default means the facts in your case were not litigated.

This process server now sat in the back row on an antiquated, wooden bench that populated the hot, muggy court room. Both Sam and his process server wore full beards, as if to hide their identity. I thought, "The process server didn't testify in court today. So, why is he here?"

Act I

The Inciting Incident

I remember, the warmth of the room in the small office where I worked. I remember, my brow broke out in sweat from the sun burning down from the high atrium like ceiling crawling with spiders. I squirmed in my black office chair feeling uncomfortable as my thoughts turned to why I was earning so little at a part-time job after working hard all of my life; so many degrees.

I thought of Sam. I had no idea what his voice sounded like. Then, I did it! I called him. He answered with a soft, raspy voice,

- "Who is this?"

I said,

- "Sam, come forward …"

…and then hung up. My heart pounded. I couldn't sit, so I urgently escaped the side of the vine-drenched building where I spent so much time on the phone trying to find better employment. My heart raced, and I did it again. I called him.
Sam started inquisitively,

- "Who is this?"

My throat choked while I thought of my mother who had recently passed.

- "Sam, I paid your small claims judgment with money my mom left me when she died. You didn't deserve my mother's money."

He hung up.

Shaken, I wandered back to my intimate office in time to greet a colleague bobbing his head above my small cubicle. I greeted him, "Hi. How was your week-end?" He gleefully responded, "Oh great! I had a great week-end at two parties with friends." We continued to chat about nothing until he strutted away. I longed for a life of friends and fun. But, when I finished work, I went home and worked all night and week-ends. I lived the life of a hamster on a spinning wheel.

The afternoon dragged, and I thought about Billy and my friend who recently died. For the last year of my friend's life, we hung out a lot. One cool night Billy stopped by our local hang out and the next day, I did an internet search on him. That's when Sam's picture popped up as working for him.

After work, I then drove to the office building where they worked. I walked up the short steps and opened the glass door slowly. I expected to greet Billy, but a man with white hair greeted me instead. I inquired, "Is Billy here?" He laughed "and explained, "There are 3 Billy's in town." I didn't see anyone else. I hadn't seen Sam for 6 years. I left a message for him to call me and left. My intent was to beg Sam to come forward about the facts of our rear-end auto accident.

After I left, on the sidewalk stood a young, tall, blondish boy with glasses talking on his phone. Spontaneously, I inquired, "Are you Sam?" "No," he responded. I then drove away.

Two days later, upon arriving home from work, my tenants informed me, "the Sherriff was here looking for you." To avoid embarrassment, I called them. The Sherriff explained, "We have to serve you with a Temporary Restraining Order (TRO)." I ensured them, "I'll pick it up."

I read, she called me every 6 months for 6 years. My mind raced, "What? No, I didn't. Oh my god, not again!"

Act II

The Temporary Restraining Order (TRO)

Driving home inattentively from the Sherriff's office, my analytical mind questioned, "How can a judge issue a restraining order, even a temporary one, which strips a person of their 2nd Amendment rights without providing them an opportunity to be heard?"

I heard Caleb's technical lecture from a class I took at City College on Search Engine Optimization (SEO) in my mind. He informed us, "…the government and legal reporting companies have the highest search priorities with Google." Great!

Doesn't the judge know? How could she hurt me based solely on the words of a boy with no evidence? Therefore, I filed a 170.6 motion to disqualify her.

Later, on Tuesday morning, before traveling to work, I stopped at the court to check on my Fee Waiver I filed after a clerk instructed me," You have to pay $400 to file your opposition against Sam's temporary restraining order." Therefore, while waiting, I decided to read the now public record of Sam's allegations. I hadn't read it before giving my paperwork to my attorney friend Frank.

When I did, my blood ran cold. Distressed, I called Frank distressed, "…did you even read the paperwork?" The allegations included:

1. I discovered where he worked and would call once every 6 months.
2. I threatened him many times in many places.
3. I sexually harassed many women and offered to pay them.
4. Throughout the last six years, I sent him ominous messages online
5. Referring to his process server who did not testify, Sam claimed 7-years after I was served with his small claims law suit, for which he wasn't present, "When she was served… tried to pull him inside her house repeatedly threatening to kill him."
6. I threatened Sam's process server with a gun.
7. My boyfriend was going to shoot the process server." I had no boyfriend.

I told Frank

"It's amazing. I called Sam once and he wasn't at the office when I stopped to see my friend Billy, which was my legal right." I told him, "I don't have $400 to defend myself. Did the police even speak to Sam's boss, Billy?" Frank had previously informed me, "Sam made no allegations; you should do nothing."

The time for the trial regarding the fee waiver was then inadvertently changed without notice to us. But luckily, Frank arrived at court early to find our trial beginning. He immediately requested a continuance until I arrived. Even so, the new judge ("ROJudge") applied the wrong standard for my fee waiver and my attorney friend just sat there. I checked box 3, not box 1 as ROJudge claimed.

Apparently, Frank didn't know the laws in criminal court as a criminal attorney. A few days later, he withdrew as my attorney. Now, I wonder if he knew what was about to happen. Later, ROJudge mischaracterized why Frank requested a continuance in his ruling.

A few days later, I woke up feeling anxious and immediately turned to look at my cell phones on my dresser. They would prove I didn't call Sam every 6 months, over 6 years. I put them in my purse and left to meet my scheduled appointment with the investigating officer regarding my request that they look at my phones.

As I moved my old car thru my neighborhood, a police car going the opposite direction appeared. A stocky, brunette, female officer motioned for me to stop. Fear gripped me. She got out of her police car and swaggered up to my window; walking as if her guns were too big for her body. There she stood, looming at my window. "Do you have a gun," she asked. I responded, "No" and inquired, "Why are you stopping me?" She instructed, "Follow me to the police station." I explained, "I am heading there for an appointment." Curious, I inquired, "What is this about?" She instructed, "Follow me."

Once parked, I walked up several flights of stairs to a white, antiquated police station. I entered while looking back to see the female officer in tow. She instructed me, "Sit down." A male officer then smashed thru another door to announce, "You're under arrest." I squawked, "I didn't drive on the street Sam works and lives. I didn't call him again"

The officer escorted me to an interrogation room. While we walked, I told him, "I never even picked up a gun." I told him, "My college boyfriend Rick was shot by his younger brother.

The story was, Rick, who was 19 at the time, and his brother had gotten into a fight. When his 15 year old brother said, "I hate you. I wish you were dead, "Rick brought out his gun, put it on the table and said, "Shoot me". …and his brother did at close range.

I despairingly told the officer, "I didn't threaten a process-server 7-years ago with a gun. There is nothing in his police report from 7-years ago about a gun. My opposing 7-year old police report tells a different story. I alleged, the process server trespassed on my property and I pushed him off. I had that legal right."

The Interrogation

We walked into the interrogation room that looked like a sound room. I sat on a little chair next to an equally small desk. My interrogator was in his mid-30s with a somewhat rugged face with deep, brown eyes that were warm and cruel at the same time. He asked, "Do you want a Public Defender?" I thought, do I have to wait hours? I then waved my Miranda rights assuming he would tell me what I did wrong. Instead, he asked, "Did you mail this?" …pointing to an empty envelope, containing a certified postage stamp. I responded, "Yes, but, what did I do wrong?"

He brought out the temporary restraining order and read small print from the top of the page, "Do not mail." In disbelief, I responded, "really, that is why I'm here, because I mailed my opposition to Sam's temporary restraining order by certified mail." My hot tears hit my face that was leathered from dealing with what I call the Machine for a decade.

The officer said with a cutting tone, "you are quite a passionate person." I agree, but I didn't say that. He looked at the envelope as if I sent something damaging out of passion.

Immediately, my psychic switched to survival mode; a state I am good at as a result of growing up on the poor side of life. I sat taller, stating strongly, "I didn't send that envelope out of passion. I sent it, because I thought I was legally required to serve Sam with my opposition."

He rose and gave me my cell phone. He then left. While I waited, my phone rang. It was the licensed lie detector company I contacted. On Forensic files and other police shows, they accept the validity of lie detector tests, so, I assumed the police would as well. I spoke about rates and made an appointment when the officer stomped back into the room. I realized later that the police probably leave your phone on purpose hoping you will call a friend to admit guilt, while still being recorded and Mirandized.

He continued to speak about Sam's allegations as if they were true. He said, "You have been calling him every 6 months?" I asked, "Where was he when I allegedly called? What were the numbers? Did you ask him one validating question?" No, the police presumed me guilty per se.

Finally, he announced, "I have to take you to jail." I was being arrested after the 14 days when the temporary restraining order should had legally expired without a right to be heard in 21 days, as required by law FRCP: Rule 65 Part 2. Title 7. 527.6 (g). It had 2 months since the temporary restraining order had been issued, and I had not been allowed one opportunity to be heard.

I begged, "What can I do? Do the police respect lie detector tests?" He said, "Yes." I then asked, "Can I take one now. Do you have one?" He responded, "No!" The stocky, female officer who escorted me to the police station, then stumbled into the room. The male officer commanded her as if she were a child.

The short, brunette officer moved her hand around the waistline of my black, summer skirt. Once done, the male officer handcuffed me. My arms ached from the cold, hard handcuffs burning into my wrists. My skin is allergic to metal.

I asked the officer, "Can you put me in a car where no one will see." He responded, "The cars are in back." He escorted me to the police parking lot and opened the door to a petite, white SUV. I smirked, "what if you are a big? He responded, "We have different sized vehicles."

As we drove, I interrogated him, "how is it that someone can have their right to own a gun taken away with no notice or right to heard and no reasonable police investigation - against someone with no criminal history – someone who has never owned a gun - without one witness or evidence of a threat, based only on a boy's word? The 2nd Amendment requires a standard of strict scrutiny."

I inquired, "Don't you know? "Internet trolls immediately publish all legal things about you, whether you are innocent or not." He responded, "There is no requirement to notify you before a temporary restraining order can issue against you."

I'm not sure who signed the order to put me in jail, but, it must have been ROJudge, which is relevant later.

You're Under Arrest

When we arrived at the county jail, the officer parked in the sun to fill out his report. Sweat streamed down my face until he opened my door. There, I stood in front of a large, looming building while the officer checked his phone. I hoped he would verify my story that Billy was the owner of the company Sam worked for. Finally, after waiting an hour in pain, he escorted me to see the nurse. I revealed to her several injuries.

He then escorted me thru the cold, metallic jail. When we stopped in front of a heavy door with a small window, the officer commanded, "Stand in the painted circle on the right of the door." Then, he opened it and pushed me in. I tripped into a large room with a metal bench stretching along the backside; a toilet and sink in one corner; and a phone, graffiti, and a bail bonds board on the other. I immediately felt claustrophic. I thought of the time my brother locked me in a toy box. Panic jolted me.

Boiling over with anxiety, I picked up the phone to call a friend," Get me out of here! Please, now. I'll pay you." Ultimately, my family friend Phil paid my bail. I had money to pay my own bail, but there is no process to pay your own bail. You need someone from the outside. It turned out the police arrested me on a Friday, which meant I had to spend a week-end in jail before seeing a judge, if I couldn't make bail. …a common practice by our police.

The smell of the toilet attacked my nose. It smelled like it hadn't been cleaned in months. Next to it were old milk cartons, open female pads, and untouched sandwiches. I spoke briefly to a young teenage girl. She expressed, "I had a fight with my boyfriend, but this time I hit the son of a bitch back."

Then, I spoke to an older, white, homeless woman. She told me, "I have bone marrow cancer and because I refused chemo, my benefits were cut. Now, I keep getting arrested for sleeping in the wrong place. Look at these fines. How do they think I can pay them? I'm homeless." I thought, "I wish I had a pen and paper."

Hours later, a guard opened the big, heavy door. "It's time to go," I thought. But, he took me to another room and asked me to sign a form before finger-printing me. I said, "Why should I be forced to sign paperwork while in jail?"

Minutes later, back in my cell, another guard opened the door and threw me a bologna sandwich and carton of milk. I asked, "Can I have a glass of water? The sink is too dirty to use."

The guard snarled, "You are in jail." …"which means I can't have a glass of water," I thought. I sat down with my disgusting meal, took one sip and threw it on the pile in the corner. My tongue moved dryly over my teeth.

Another guard came to manipulate me, "If you provide me with all the contact information of those who are close to you, you may get out early." Now, as I reflect, I don't trust the Machine knowing who is close to me. As I have observed over the years in my town, women who have been disenfranchised the most with no compassion, appear to be the most vulnerable with assets (i.e. older, single, white middle-class women who own real estate).

More time passed before another guard escorted me down the hall to the changing room for women remaining in jail. He commanded me, "Go in." Instead, I gripped the door frame tightly, emphasizing, "No, my bail is paid." Another guard joined in to push me in the room, explaining loudly, "if you don't cooperate, we will file another charge against you." Really! Later, the bail bonds told me, if you don't cooperate they keep you all night.

They pushed me into a large bathroom. Two of the women inside, were removed from the other area 3 hours earlier. One was the woman with bone cancer. I inquired, "Have you been in here for the past three hours laying on this filthy, hard floor?" She acknowledged, "Yes." A male officer sat at a window facing in. It reminded me of the Red Light District in Holland.

A blanket was hung to serve as a curtain to give little privacy for women to change into their prison outfits while the male guard looked on. I pulled the blanket down and put it on the floor, so we didn't have to sit on the dirty floor. Finally, a guard opened the door and took me back to my original holding cell. So far, I had been in the county jail for 7 hours.

For the entire 9 hours in jail, I didn't pee once. It was too dirty. Again, I positioned myself at the door and small window, because the bench was occupied with sleeping girls.

As I reflected on my current situation, I thought of the time as a young woman when I was kidnapped from a downtown city by 4 young black men. One of those 4 poor boys then saved my life while committing a crime he was probably forced into by his friends and economic circumstances. Yet, here I sat in jail as a result of what was generally a no fault auto accident with a boy who claimed I was solely responsible for it, and a court who thought it was OK to deny me one opportunity to prove my innocence before throwing my career under the bus.

Then, with a claustrophobic driven nausea, as a ruse, I turned to the sleeping girls and said, "Hey the button is broken, referring to the intercom button – my only communication with my captors." As I continued to press the button in rapid succession, one girl spat, "stupid pigs." The other berated me, "Shut the Fuck Up." But, I continued my rant. An officer on the other side then finally spit out, "we only respond to medical conditions."

Ah ha! Finally, a way out! Immediately, with determination, I pushed that button again to declare, "My foot hurts. I need a doctor." 10 minutes later, the door opened. I was being released at almost 10 pm. I spent 9 hours in jail.

A tall, looming, female guard escorted me to their counter to sign papers. Security cameras were everywhere. This woman terrorized me by stating, "I would like to keep you." A male guard then grabbed my arm, walked me through two large sliding doors and thrust me into a dark parking lot on a secluded road; at night with no car or anyone waiting for me.

I turned to the building that loomed behind me and yelled, "Fuck You. You Son of a Bitch! Fuck You" The large, lifeless building that represented the cold-hearted Machine, dominated the night sky, illuminated with bright stars. But, how can our government (the Machine) dump women out into the night? 15 minutes later, my friend picked me up in my car. I was so mad.

A few days later, on my quest to accumulate all my paperwork, I strolled into the police station to get a copy of their report, but the Machine told me No. '

This is wrong. A person should have a right to all evidence against them, including the police report, the audio from the interrogation, the order signed by the judge who sent you to jail, etc.; just as your attorney and public defender would.

Criminal Court

Tuesday came fast. My trial for criminal court was set for the morning, which meant I had to miss another day of work. From across the room, I saw Jane. When I approached her to say hi, she told me, "Shh." Whispering, she told me, "The DA put charges against me, as well as another woman who fought to save her home, like me."

All of us women who have been brutally beaten up for fighting known mortgage fraud are older, white, middle-class women. Jane was being prosecuted for minor things she did to save her home, which she lost. In contrast, no banker ever faced one charge in our town. …and I don't know anyone who received money from the settlements Kamala Harris claims to have fought for.

I walked into court with the memory of my ordeal in jail. After about an hour, a man from the public defender's office sat down next to me and began to read Sam's allegations to justify his restraining order." Fear and shame dominated my senses as he read the allegations. I now wonder if an attorney advised Sam on how to meet the elements for a temporary restraining order. One element is continuity. ***What I did, didn't fulfill this element without embellishment.***

This public defender asked me, "Do you want to plead guilty? You can be excused quickly if you do." I responded bitterly, "No!" He asked, "Do you want a trial?" …and convinced me not to. Now, I wish I had. I would had challenged the underlying temporary restraining order itself, which was my right. How can I violate a temporary restraining order that didn't meet the elements to be issued in the first place?

I went several times to the court to retain a public defender. I didn't really trust them, but I had no choice. I didn't have the money to hire an attorney at $300+ an hour. Finally, a woman called. Her name was Sally. When I called Sally with questions later, she rebelled, "I'm busy. I have a lot of cases." If a public defender ever says that to you, remind them that is not your problem. Their responsibility is to help you."

At the 2nd criminal trial, while sitting in the lobby, Sally came over and asked, "What are you doing here? Why aren't you in court?" Sally then tried to cut me a deal with the prosecutor, as my outrage spilled over; transformed by fear of being falsely accused of atrocities. Court procedures that deny the vulnerable one chance to be heard appears to be a pattern in all the cases.

Finally, after four attempts, Sally negotiated a deal I could live with, which was, if I didn't contact Sam for 2 months, the DA would dismiss all charges. I was ready to go to trial.

Before leaving, I requested, "I want to make a statement on the record." She looked at me with disdain and addressed the court, "Christy wants to make a statement on the record." My criminal judge confirmed, "I won't make a ruling."

I walked up to the podium to proclaim, "My public defender assured me that it is my 1st Amendment constitutional right to speak out. Also, I wouldn't recognize Sam outside the court room."

As we left, I inquired, "Where can I get a copy?" She pointed and I parted, "Good bye," moving quickly up the stairs. A young, pretty, blond woman was sitting at the counter. I inquired, "Can I get a copy of the audio from my criminal trial today?" She glanced at me bewildered, looking at her computer, she announced, "the audio isn't on." Determined, I went back to court, walked up to the podium and let the judge know. The judge instructed his clerks, "…check the audio. Is it working?" I then made my statement a 2nd time.

Walking swiftly again to the young woman's counter, I requested, "Can I now have a copy?" She again looked bewilder, "Nothing was recorded," she uttered. I complained, "Unbelievable!" Exhausted, I walked one more time up to the podium to powerfully announce, "The audio still isn't working." The Sherriff coincidentally declared, "I have batteries." Once his task was completed, I made my statement a 3rd time.

Lie Detector Test

A few days later, I called the licensed lie detector company, even though I didn't have the money. My phone call to Sam already cost me bail, several days off work and more stress, but maybe my little "who" voice will be heard some day.

I drove south and walked up to an office building, decorated with old fashion, wooden décor. I waited until a fashion-minded, young woman sat me down on a cold, hard, metal chair. The lie detector expert started by asking me questions to establish a baseline. He chimed, "most often, men come in here when they are unjustly accused."

He put a large strap across my chest, a tight attachment on my finger and a strap across my back. He asked, "Have you ever lied to a cop?" Did you phone Sam every 6 months over the past 6 years?" I passed all questions as expected. The expert ended, "its $350 for 3 questions." Later, I emailed the results to the police thinking it would matter. But, it didn't. I was guilty per se.

Could it be that TV shows who accept lie detector tests do so to misrepresent to the public that our justice system is fair, when it is not?

Armed with my new evidence, since I never had ONE day in court to dispute Sam's allegations for his restraining order, I scheduled an ex-parte hearing. It seemed important to dispute the temporary restraining order before a hearing to make it permanent. I properly served Sam. As a result, he was present in court. But, ROJudge did not even come out. Instead, he sent his secretary to read his order, which began by falsely claiming I had not served Sam. I felt over-whelmed.

Finally, my day in court.

Finally, it was time for me to have my one opportunity to challenge Sam's allegations. Do you think after being arrested for mailing my opposition to Sam's restraining order by certified mail from the post office, I would get a fair hearing?

To recap, it was claimed in Sam's initial police report:

1. I discovered where he worked and would call once every 6 months.
2. I threatened him many times in many places.
3. I sexually harassed many women and offered to pay them.

4. Throughout the last six years, I sent him ominous messages online
5. Referring to his process server who did not testify, Sam claimed 7-years after I was served with his small claims law suit, for which he wasn't present, "When she was served… tried to pull him inside her house repeatedly threatening to kill him."
6. I threatened Sam's process server with a gun.
7. My boyfriend threatened to shoot the processes server." I had no boyfriend.

None of this is mentioned in the 7-year old police report by the process server. …all this is part of my public record today.

I woke up early at 5 am. The hearing to make the temporary restraining order permanent was scheduled for 9:30 am. By 10, my 4 witnesses had arrived. I sat next to my friends when a court clerk handed me ROJudge's initial ruling. As I read, I couldn't breathe. He claimed I hadn't filed 1 opposition, when I filed 3 as events kept happening.

I thought, "The fix is in," and reflected on an incident. I remembered while waiting for an attorney. I remember, I sat in the corner of his little office piled high with papers. As he focused on his work, he spontaneously instructed his secretary, "Get the judge on the line. I want to talk about this case before we file it." His eyes then fell on me and he gulped. His admission has remained with me.

Is the winner of a case known before it is filed?

Anxious, I turned to my one friend and requested, "Here is $10. Go get a copy of the court docket from records upstairs." A few minutes later, she came back with a copy of the docket proving I filed three oppositions.

Remember, ROJudge signed the order to put me in jail for mailing my opposition to Sam's temporary restraining order. ROJudge also misrepresented that

I had to pay $400 to file my opposition. The clerk misspoke and I was able to file it without payment. It's interesting, later the court moved the records department away from the hearing rooms.

Just as important, ROJudge made another amazing statement in his initial ruling, which was, "since the 1st judge issued a temporary restraining order, it must be right." But, remember, I was never given one chance to be heard and no reasonable police investigation was done. I wasn't even contacted. Judges routinely propagate such unconstitutional rulings.

At 9:30, ROJudge called my case. I began,

- "I have a copy of the court docket from upstairs. I filed three oppositions. I filed all with proper proof of service, proper affidavits and requests for judicial notice for all three of them. And I have stamped copies of all of that. Yet, your tentative says I filed no responses."

He sputtered,

- "Let's reschedule this case so I can read everything."

I objected,

- "your honor, I request a continuance. I have witnesses who can't stay until the afternoon."

ROJudge barked,

- "it is rescheduled for this afternoon."

I was given NO choice but to have a hearing without my witnesses being present. In other words, my due process rights were again violated.

The Afternoon Hearing

As the afternoon sun gleaned thru the mosaic windows of the court, I moved closer to the long table to speak into the microphone to cross-examine Sam. I tried to object when he made statements that I claim were untrue, but ROJudge blocked my constitutional right.

- "…Christy is going to make every effort not to interrupt you."

I rebelled,

- "He is not answering my questions."

"I have a right to object," I thought. Sam went on,

- "Yes… I do not claim that Christy called me on the phone …the police misstated …that is just a discrepancy … I claim she contacted me every six months …."

I cleared my throat,

- "Sam, you make a claim that I threatened you many places, many times. Can you name one place where I threatened you, one place, one time?"

ROJudge assisted,

- "Did you see her person to person?"

Sam responded,

- "Not since the last time in court your Honor, but I have been contacted through Google, LinkedIn, Facebook, Gmail."

I attempted to get clarification

- "..as I understand it, he just testified that he never saw me in person."

ROJudge responded

- "He said, no, you hadn't seen him in person."

Still, I needed clarification

- "So I just want to verify … he has not seen me in person in the last five years before April…"

ROJudge barked

- "I got that in my mind, indelibly."

…2011? - not 6 months ago, over 6 years. I continued my cross examination,

- "what email do you have to substantiate your allegations that I contacted you thru the Internet every six months?"

He responded,

- "I don't have any other email…."

I confirmed,

- "The only evidence he has is from 5 years ago."

Both emails have the same basic content - my money offer for witnesses to come forward regarding our auto accident, Sam testified,

- "You threatened me through them."

I argued in my opposition,

- "There is no evidence of a threat to Sam. My two 5-year-old Face book emails were to a few of his public friends offering money for a witness to our auto accident to come forward, while I was in litigation with Sam. These email do not meet the element of 'individual' for a temporary restraining order. CCP §§ 2017 reads: "… discovery is permissible if the requested information is…is relevant to …pending action…."

I took my case with Sam to the U.S. Supreme Court. But, even though the issues in the case could affect many pro per litigants – the most vulnerable, the court refused to hear it. Finding a witness to an accident was relevant to my litigation 5 years earlier with Sam. I inquired, referring to Sam's only email evidence,

- "It is from 5 years ago, right?"

He responded,

- "Correct…."

In other words, Sam kept two five-year old emails, but didn't keep ONE other digital communication he claims I sent him every 6 months for 6 years.

But, these admissions by Sam under oath won't be part of the public record if ROJudge rules in favor of Sam. In other words, my public record will suggest that his accusations, even though Sam admits under oath that most relevant facts that gave rise to his temporary restraining order were a discrepancy, and the process server didn't testify.

The court continued,

➤ "Do you have any witnesses?"

Sam responded,

➤ "No."

Sam never called one witness even though he testified in his initial police report about what happened to his process server 7-years ago and brought this same process server to court. …which according to ROJudge is hearsay.

In contrast, when I attempted to use the same police report ROJudge blasted in his final ruling about Sam's allegations regarding his process server 7 years earlier, to secure his restraining order in the first place, ROJudge intervened,

➤ "The police report is not acceptable in evidence because … we consider hearsay …is denied."

The Hearsay Rule

But, what is hearsay? Its definition is, "a statement that was made *other than* by a witness testifying at the trial; offered to prove the truth of the content of the statement."

In my case, Sam wasn't a witness when his process server served me 7-years ago at my home with his small claims lawsuit over our auto accident. Yet, Sam offered his testimony in his police report about what happened to someone else..

To be sarcastic, if this isn't hearsay, I don't know what is?

Even more basic, hearsay is hearsay; no matter its application. Evidence (i.e. the police report) can't be considered not hearsay in a trial to take away your 2nd Amendment right to bear arms thru a temporary restraining order without a right to be heard or notified, yet then be considered hearsay for the trial to make the temporary restraining order permanent.

This use by the court flip flops their application of the hearsay rule, which denies you due process to challenge the evidence used to issue the temporary restraining order in the first place.

Do you get it? Hearsay is like a mathematical equation. $1 + 1 = 2$; no matter its application. Evidence can't be NOT hearsay one day, and then hearsay the next, based on the type of trial.

I should have been given my constitutional right to challenge the same evidence the court used to issue the temporary restraining order during the trial to make it permanent, whether I subpoenaed the police or not. The police officer who took the initial report was not at the 1st hearing that took away my 2nd Amendment rights. No one was there …and that's the point!

Act III

ROJudge ended the trial testifying after the court reporter had stopped transcribing, "what's the big deal, many people have restraining orders against them" …and this is the attitude of judges toward our 2nd Amendment rights.

ROJudge's ruling represented Sam's claim about his process server 7-years earlier, even though it was hearsay evidence and the process server did not testify, and how Sam supposedly won his case against me regarding our rear-end auto accident 7-years ago, for which all this arises; ignoring that Sam won a small claims Default judgment.

After all the admissions Sam called discrepancies under oath, ROJudge's ruling should had been amazing to me. But, after all the gross misrepresentations ROJudge made during this process, including the requirement that I pay $400, and his initial ruling that I filed 1 response, when I had filed 3; his ruling was not a shock.

I appealed ROJudge's ruling on many grounds. When I requested the Transcript for my appeal, I was only given the transcript from the afternoon. I had to assertively request a copy of the transcript from the morning trial where ROJudge grossly misrepresented facts in his initial ruling and rescheduled my hearing to deny me my right to have witnesses heard.

I drove to personally file my Notice and Motion of Appeal, Affidavit, Request for Judicial Notice, and Proof of Service. My intent was to have stamped copies of all my filings when the appellate court pulled their usual trick of claiming I hadn't filed something; losing another day of work. The Proof of Service is the most lied about document by our courts. But, that's another essay.

…and as expected, the appellate court did claim I did not file a Proof of Service. This misrepresentation kept my documents from being placed on the record for the public to see. Now, the court can claim my appeal was harassment, rather than the truth – I did file a Proof of Service with all of my documents personally, yet the court denied me my due process rights based on their misrepresentation.

What About the Default Judgment

After reading ROJudge's order, which referenced Sam winning his case with me 7 years ago over our auto accident, I learned that Sam's small claims Default order is not in the public record for my case. Default means the facts in your case were not litigated. This Default judgment was fundamental to my case with Sam 6 years ago, because the judge ruled I had relitigated when I didn't.

Therefore, I complained to the Judicial Performance Committee that the order signed by the only authority in my case, the private attorney who acted as a small claims judge 7 years ago, is not on the public record. The order of entry, on the public record, is only signed by a court clerk.

The court responded to my complaint by writing, "The Order is stamped Confidential per court procedures and is not public." Really?! The court procedures are set by the court, and the small claims judge is the same judge who protected Sam in my case 7 years ago by ignoring that his judgment was Default. She incorrectly applied the term relitigation. In other words, the legal character of my case was changed by the judge hiding the fact that Sam's judgment was Default.

Why would an Order be stamped Confidential, but to hide the court's corruption? What is the court hiding by making the small claims Default judgment (Order) Confidential? … That their ruling to protect Sam at all costs was unjust?

As a result of the order being hidden, all subsequent judges ignored the fact that I didn't have one opportunity to oppose Sam's allegations, regarding our rear end auto accident 7 years earlier. The legal character of my case was changed, which has caused me over $1,000,000 worth of damage.

The Back Story: Seven Years Earlier

7-years earlier, on a balmy fall afternoon, I stopped partially in my street to open my car door to collect my dog, when I saw him running toward me, before rushing my minor child to class.

While in park, I allege Sam backed out of my neighbor's driveway where he was turning around and backed into my car. Such accidents are generally no fault.

A few weeks passed, when I answered a knock on my office door. A 6' man I didn't recognize aggressively approached me and I pushed him. I demanded, "What are you doing on my property." He responded, "You are served." I then pushed him when I heard my big dog growl from inside, instructing, "Get off my property. This is private property." We both then filed a police report. No allegations of a gun were alleged.

On the day of the small claims hearing, I put on my white beanie hat to prepare to ride my bike to court in the cold morning air. I had sold my car after the accident with Sam. I arrived 5 minutes late. Even so, Sam received a hearing in record time with a private attorney acting as the small claims judge. I didn't see anyone else waiting to be heard.

In contrast, the common man waits for hours to have their small claims cases heard in crowded court rooms. 5 minutes meant I lost my case. The order signed, clearly states, Default.

I then filed a motion to set aside Sam's judgment. Generally, a motion to set aside a judgment does not allow for a trial the same day as the motion is heard. I packed up my evidence and called my witness before leaving the house, "Hello, are you coming to court?" He responded, "I have to work. I'll be 5 minutes away. Call me." But, the female attorney serving as the small claims judge, told me, "…you were served. It was your fault you were late," and sustained Sam's judgment without providing me with ONE opportunity to be heard.

Today, her order is also not on the public record for my case. Why, because it confirms that Sam won a Default judgment, and the court goal is to hide that fact from the public.

1 year later, Sam filed a DMV report. Therefore, since Sam's judgment was Default and no issues litigated, I filed in Superior Court. I remember, after paying my previous family law attorney to review my opposition, I called Sam's attorney

to offer to settle "I can only afford $50 a month right now, but will increase when able." I heard, "I would rather go after your house."

…and isn't that what all of this is really about. My career would not had been damaged if I hadn't worked so hard in my life to own a home in a nice place. In my wealthy town, older, middle-class, white women were targeted by the bankers – there is no doubt!

Subsequently, Sam's attorney filed a motion to ask the court to rule 9 of my previous, unrelated cases against primarily banks for known mortgage fraud held to be adverse against me to keep me from litigating without first paying $15,000. This motion is used 90% of the time by insurance companies and banks.

The judge that was responsible for the Default judgment not being on the record, ruled that 9 of my previous, unrelated cases were adverse against me, even though 6 were 'dismissed without prejudice' with no adverse evidence or rulings.

But, a lawsuit dismissed without prejudice means that none of the rights or privileges of the individual involved are considered lost or waived. Therefore, a case dismissed without prejudice can't be presumed adverse against you without destroying the legal meaning of 'dismiss without prejudice. Yet, my career was damaged simply because I dismissed cases 6 years ago, using a judicial Form CIV-110 with NO warnings of extreme consequences 7-years in the future. 6 of my cases were older than 5 years.

The judge ignored 62 pages of evidence and 5 settlement agreements and the fact that Sam's judgment was Default, and set amazing new precedent. The Appellate court then left out the terms, 'dismiss without prejudice' and Default to sustain Sam's ruling by boldly misrepresenting the facts and evidence;" backing up the injustice, rather than overseeing the lower court properly.

Conclusion

I lost my right to own a gun, my career; and had my public internet profile and court record damaged, for what Sam called a discrepancy under oath!

As a result, I can't answer the question, what will happen to the protagonist of this story, me. Will I be able to afford to grow old after working all my life, which is what I worry about?

However, I can answer the main question here, which is: Are courts destroying the 2nd Amendment without regard to its strict scrutiny requirement? The answer is YES – in the most amazing manner.

Courts are destroying our 2nd Amendment rights thru their liberal issuance of temporary restraining orders without due process, and their perversion of the Hearsay Rule. Consequently, reform is needed for those concerned about the validity of our system today.

Without reform, I see the debate about guns this way. …if we are currently living in the Wild, Wild West where justice is for sale by a court system that has no integrity, why would people give up their guns?

… and how can we have a reasonable discussion about gun control?

My Suggestions for Court Reform

- The court can't renew a Temporary Restraining Order after 14 days, if the 21-day requirement of a hearing to challenge the evidence giving rise to it, without your right to be heard, is not scheduled.

- A defendant has an equal right to personally obtain copies of all police reports, audio of interrogations, videos from cameras, etc. – the same as their attorney or public defender would.

- All orders must be part of the public record. An Order can't be Confidential.

- A Temporary Restraining Order can't issue without the person with whom it is against, having a right to be heard and a reasonable police investigation done to confirm the accuser's allegations. An exception is only if a person has a known history of violence.

Imagine in the future, if I am ever accused of an altercation, the police would just look at the record without knowing that Sam admitted under oath that most accusations were discrepancies and assume it truthful.

- A person must be released from prison within 30 minutes after making bail and a process to pay your own bail must be put into place.
- An audio of the trial and transcript must be part of the public court record.
- A better changing condition for women in prison must be installed and only women guards can be placed to look into women's changing rooms. Also, prisoners should not be made to lay on a hard bathroom floor for hours waiting to change.

I end my story with a question that is generally part of a good story's architecture, which is, how did the protagonist grow from this conflict?

Well, after years of being defamed from fighting the Machine, I realize that I have become more of an introvert than ever before. But, it's OK, because I'm comfortable with me, and often prefer it; a state you need to be in when you speak truth to power. I don't need your approval.

….but, I wonder, what role models do our young people have? How can we expect the poor kid to be honest when our politicians aren't, our judges aren't, the police aren't – why should they be good citizens when justice is for sale?

…in the Wild, Wild West!